THE LITTLE BOOK OF MONEY

Compiled by

EVELYN STEINBERG & MARILYN WILLIAMS

A LITTLE RED BOOK

ARSENAL PULP PRESS

A little red book

THE LITTLE BOOK OF MONEY

ISBN 1-55152-011-7
CIP DATA: *see page 6*

LITTLE RED BOOKS
are published by
ARSENAL PULP PRESS
1062 HOMER STREET #100
VANCOUVER BC V6B 2W9

COVER ILLUSTRATION:
Eve Corbel
TYPESETTING: *Vancouver Desktop*
PRINTING: *Webcom*
PRINTED AND BOUND IN CANADA

TABLE OF CONTENTS

CATALOGUING IN PUBLICATION DATA

Main entry under title:
The little book of money
(A Little red book)
Includes bibliographical references and index.
ISBN1-55152-011-7
1. Money—Quotations, maxims, etc.
I. Steinberg, Evelyn, 1943- II. Williams, Marilyn, 1936- III. Series.
HG221.L57 1994 332.4 C94-910725-5

MONEY QUESTIONS

WHERE DOES MONEY START, but in *nomenclatura*? Who were Money's Adam and Eve? Who named it *specie*, who coined *the stuff*, the long green, the lean green, the folding, the ready, the *bees and honey*, the do-re-mi, the hoot, jack, kale, moolah, the needful—oh, the ever-needful, I mean the nicker, the mopus, the *ooftish*, the loot, the *pelf*, the *green* green stuff, the real spondulicks? And who gets enough of the stuff? Enough smash, enough wampum, enough whistle and toot? Enough stumpy, swag, treasure, and wad? Well, it's the high-hats who get enough of it, the mucky-mucks, the high rollers, the big wheels with their swanky big-wig pals; these are the guys who've got plenty of scratch and crackle: the suits, the kingfish, the pooh-bahs who put on the Ritz; when you're the big cheese, you're the big enchilada, you're the big noise and a big wheel and you're *oofty* because you've got the wherewithal, the *tusheroon*; you never count shekels or smackeroos, your simoleons are safe because there's always more, more *gelt* where that came from, more and more gravy, more yonga, more yuncer, more yennom and smacker; when you've got lots of oscar you've got lots of *kylege*; it's all dibs and dinero and pesos and ducats but you don't care: you've got the ace and ackers to burn. Call it beans or potatoes or sausage and mash: it's all boodle to you when you're Top Dog or Fat Cat, Top Cat or Posh.

But is it animal, mineral, vegetable, or cereal? Muckworms dream of lettuce and cabbage and duckies and bucks; they've got plenty of dough and they make good bread but they never part with their hay and keep their cake stashed carefully away. These are the cheapskates and cheese-parers, the chuffs and churls, crawfish who won't part with a clam; they keep their cod's roe in a box, they're lickpennies who've got lots of rhino but hide all the brass. Nabals and pikers, pinchpennies and scrimps, they're tight with their wads and they'll skin your flint if you don't keep your rocks in your pocket and your scramble in your bag. It's all beans, you say, but it's tender, it's legal, and it's *lucre* to boot. It's *funt*, it's *mazu-ma*, it's sugar in slabs; it's all coin of the realm, greenbacks and lolly, billies and the ever-folding—in short, the very Jimmy O'Goblin of the questions.

Money questions are as old as the species, although money answers are never easy to come by. The present volume represents an exhausting, if not exhaustive, culling of remark and commentary, retort and riposte, on this, the most ancient of puzzles.

— STEPHEN OSBORNE
SERIES EDITOR

Money: current medium of exchange in form of coins and banknotes

— *Oxford Dictionary*

Money is like manure. If you spread it around it does a lot of good. But if you pile it up in one place it stinks like hell.

— *Clint Murchison Jr., industrialist*

Money is like a sixth sense without which you cannot make a complete use of the other five.

— *William Somerset Maugham,* Of Human Bondage

Money is like honey: a little of it is sweet, but a super abundance cloys.

— *B.C. Forbes,* Epigrams

Money is like an arm and a leg—use it or lose it.

— *Henry Ford, industrialist*

When money speaks the truth is silent.

— *Russian proverb*

Money begets money.

— *John Ray*, English Proverbs

Money speaks sense in a language all nations understand.

— *Aphra Behn*, The Rover

Money doesn't talk, it swears.

— *Bob Dylan*, It's Alright, Ma

As soon as you bring up money, I notice, conversation gets sociological, then political, then moral.

— *Jane Smiley*, Good Will

You've heard money talking? Did you understand the message?

— *Marshall McLuhan,*
The Mechanical Bride

Finance is the art or science of managing revenues and resources for the best advantage of the manager.

— *Ambrose Bierce, writer*

The two most beautiful words in the English language are "check enclosed."

— New York Herald Tribune

Why does a slight tax increase cost you two hundred dollars and a substantial tax cut save you thirty cents?

— *Peg Bracken, writer*

Everybody wants to make money—but how many want it enough to work for it?

— *Roy Thomson in R. Braddon,* Roy Thomson of Fleet Street

When a man tells you that he got rich through hard work, ask him: "Whose?"

— *Don Marquis, writer*

I simply don't see the point of getting up at six all the time you are young and working eighteen hours a day in order to be a millionaire, and then when you are a millionaire still getting up at six and working eighteen hours a day. . . . What does it all mean?

— *Nancy Mitford,* Pigeon Pie

When a thing is current, it creates currency.

— *Marshall McLuhan*

For some 4,000 years prior to the 20th century, three metals were used for purposes of exchange: silver, copper, and gold.

—*from John Kenneth Galbraith,* Money: Whence It Came, Where It Went

If possible, honestly, if not, somehow, make money.

— *Horace (Quintus Horatius Flaccus),* Epistles I

To turn $100 into $110 is work. To turn $100 million into $110 million is inevitable.

— *Edgar Bronfman, industrialist*

It is remarkable . . . what a change of temper a fixed income will bring about.

— *Virginia Woolf,* A Room of One's Own

Money is the seed of money, and the first guinea is sometimes more difficult to acquire than the second million.

— *Jean Jacques Rousseau, writer*

Wealth—any income that's at least one hundred dollars more a year than the income of one's wife's sister's husband.

— *H.L. Mencken, writer*

No man but a blockhead ever wrote except for money.

— *Samuel Johnson, in James Boswell,* Life of Johnson

To think twice in every matter and follow the lead of others is no way to make money.

— *Ihara Saikaku,* The Japanese Family Storehouse; or, The Millionaires' Gospel

I never made any money 'til I took off my pants.

— *Sally Rand, dancer-entertainer*

Americans want action for their money. They are fascinated by its self-reproducing qualities.

— *Paula Nelson,* The Joy of Money

The bulls make money / The bears make money / But the pigs get slaughtered.

— *Wall Street axiom*

There is nothing wrong with men possessing riches, but the wrong comes when riches possess man.

— *Billy Graham*

There are few ways in which a man can be more innocently employed than in getting money.

— *Samuel Johnson, in James Boswell,* Life of Johnson

I cannot afford to waste my time making money.

— *Louis J.R. Agassiz, zoologist, geologist*

To force myself to earn more money,
I determined to spend more.

—*James Agate, drama critic*

To be clever enough to get a great deal of money, one must be stupid enough to want it.

— *G.K. Chesterton*

People who think money can do anything may very well be suspected of doing anything for money.

— *Mary Pettibone Poole,*
A Glass Eye at a Keyhole

If you rub up against money long enough, some of it may rub off on you.

— *Damon Runyon, "A Very Honorable Guy"*

No man will take counsel, but every man will take money.

— *Jonathan Swift*

Chief Justice: Your means are very slender and your waste is great.
Falstaff: I would it were otherwise. I would my means were greater and my waist slenderer.

— *William Shakespeare,* Henry IV

Most people seek after what they do not possess and are enslaved by the very things they want to acquire.

— *Anwar Sadat*

When poverty comes in at the door, love flies out the window.

— *17th-century maxim*

Money, it turned out, was exactly like sex, you thought of nothing else if you didn't have it and thought of other things if you did.

— *James Baldwin*, Nobody Knows My Name

Funds, not sex, are the root of human motivation.

— *Hugh Hood*, A Game of Touch

I'm tired of Love: I'm still more tired of Rhyme./But money gives me pleasure all the Time.

— *Hilaire Belloc*, Fatigue

For I don't care too much for money,
for money can't buy me love.
—*John Lennon, "Can't Buy Me Love"*

According to Suetonius, following the death of Caligula, all money bearing his likeness was called in and melted down so that not only the tyrant's name but his features would be forgotten.
—*from John Kenneth Galbraith,* Money: Whence It Came, Where It Went

Her voice is full of money.
— *F. Scott Fitzgerald,* The Great Gatsby

Money will say more in one moment than the most eloquent lover can in years.
— *Henry Fielding*

All heiresses are beautiful.

—*John Dryden*, King Arthur

If women didn't exist, all the money in the world would have no meaning.

—*Aristotle Onassis*

Gold and love affairs are difficult to hide.

—*Spanish proverb*

Money is a good servant, but a bad master.

— *Sir Francis Bacon*

Money is a terrible master but an excellent servant.

— *P.T. Barnum*

So you think that money is the root of all evil? Have you ever asked what is the root of money?

— *Ayn Rand*, Atlas Shrugged

Money is the fruit of evil as often as the root of it.

— *Henry Fielding*

What I have here is a complete indictment of our present-day society, our whole world. What's wrong with it is money, honey, money.

— *Margaret Walker, in Claudia Tate,* Black Women Writers at Work

What is the matter with the poor is poverty; what is the matter with the rich is uselessness.

— *George Bernard Shaw*

Money may be the husk of many things, but not the kernel. It brings you food, but not appetite; medicine, but not health; acquaintances, but not friends; servants, but not happiness; days of joy, but not peace or happiness.

— *Henrik Ibsen*

Wine maketh merry: but money answereth all things.

— *Ecclesiastes, X.19*

In America, money takes the place of God.

— *Anzia Yezierska,*
Red Ribbon on a White Horse

The dollar sign is the only sign in which the modern man appears to have any real faith.

— *Helen Rowland,* Reflections of a Bachelor Girl

In God we trust, all others pay cash.

— *Sign used in retail stores during the Great Depression*

Counterfeiting goes back at least to 540 B.C., when Polycrates of Samos is said to have cheated the Spartans with coins of simulated gold.

—*from John Kenneth Galbraith,* Money: Whence It Came, Where It Went

If you want to know what God thinks of money, look at the people he gives it to.

— *New England maxim*

The silk suit cost me much money, and I pray to God to make me able to pay for it.

— *Samuel Pepys*

When it is a question of money, everybody is of the same religion.

— *Voltaire*

Make money your God, and it will plague you like the devil.

— *Henry Fielding*

When I had money everyone called me brother.

— *Polish proverb*

The world is his who has money to go over it.

— *Ralph Waldo Emerson, "Fate"*

Now that he was rich, he was not thought ignorant any more, but simply eccentric.

— *Mavis Gallant,*
The Pegnitz Junction

He had so much money that he could afford to look poor.

— *Edgar Wallace*

People who know how much they're worth aren't usually worth that much.

— *Nelson Bunker Hunt, billionaire*

No one would remember the Good Samaritan if he'd only had good intentions. He had money as well.

— *Margaret Thatcher*

Riches do not make one rich but busy.

— *Fernando de Rojas,* La Celestina

To be rich is no longer a sin; it's a miracle.

— *Hand-stitched pillow pictured in* Vogue

A rich man is also an unusual man, and a great financier is as rare a creature as a great painter.

— *Robertson Davies,* Moonbeams from the Larger Lunacy

There's no reason to be the richest man in the cemetery. You can't do any business from there.

— *Colonel Sanders*

[The rich] are indeed rather possessed by their money than possessors.

— *Robert Burton,* The Anatomy of Melancholy

A man is rich in proportion to the number of things which he can afford to let alone.

— *Henry David Thoreau,* Walden

—You know, Ernest, the rich are much different from us.
—Yes, I know. They have more money.

— *F. Scott Fitzgerald and Ernest Hemingway*

If you can count your money, you don't have a billion dollars.

— *J. Paul Getty, billionaire*

The only way not to think about money is to have a great deal of it.

— *Edith Wharton,* The House of Mirth

The ruling class isn't dissatisfied: they're healthy, well-fed, live in beauty, enjoy their importance: fun-loving cannibals.

— *Marge Piercy,* Sisterhood is Powerful

It is the wretchedness of being rich that you have to live with rich people.

— *Logan Pearsall Smith, essayist*

After the rich, the most obnoxious people in the world are those who serve the rich.

— *Edna O'Brien,*
August is a Wicked Month

Some people's money is merited /
And other people's is inherited.

— *Ogden Nash, "The Terrible People"*

Some people think they are worth a lot of money just because they have it.

— *Fanny Hurst, writer*

The man who dies rich, dies disgraced.

— *Andrew Carnegie, philanthropist*

Money creates taste.

— *Jenny Holtzer, artist,* Truisms

There are people who have money and people who are rich.

— *Coco Chanel, fashion designer*

I don't like money, actually, but it quiets my nerves.

— *Joe Louis, boxer*

If I was honest, I would admit that money is one half of happiness; it makes it so much more attractive.

— *Marie Lenru,* Journal

I've been rich and I've been poor; rich is better.

— *Sophie Tucker, singer*

I didn't want to be rich, I just wanted enough to get the couch reupholstered.

— *Kate Mostel*

In my book, anyone pretending he has no interest in money is either a fool or a knave.

— *Leslie Ford,* Invitation to Murder

On every economic level, the meaning of money is significantly different for men than for women.

—*Andrea Dworkin, activist*

Money demands that you sell, not your weakness to men's stupidity, but your talent to their reason.

—*Ayn Rand,* Atlas Shrugged

Since men have used women's 'beauty' as a form of currency in circulation among men, ideas about 'beauty' have evolved since the Industrial Revolution side by side with ideas about money, so that the two are virtual parallels in our consumer economy.

— *Naomi Wolf, writer*

We women ought to put first things first. Why should we mind if men have their faces on the money, as long as we get our hands on it.

— *Ivy Baker Priest, U.S. Treasurer,*
Green Grows Ivy

A boy spends his sperm and his money on women. A man uses his sperm and his women to produce wealth.

— *Andrea Dworkin, activist*

If one is rich and one's a woman, one can be quite misunderstood.

— *Katherine Graham, publisher*

Men always try to keep women out of business so they won't find out how much fun it really is.

— *Vivien Kellems, industrialist*

If you have money, sister, don't deny it, share it.

— *Rita Mae Brown, writer*

When I wish I was rich, then I know I am ill.

— *D.H. Lawrence*

The power of money is distinctly a male power.

— *Andrea Dworkin, activist*

There are many to whom money has no personal appeal, but who can be tempted by the power it confers.

— *Agatha Christie,* Crooked House

Liking money like I like it, it is nothing less than mysticism. Money is a glory.

— *Salvador Dali*

Discovery and conquest set in motion a vast flow of precious metal from America to Europe, and the result was a huge increase in prices. In Andalusia, between 1500 and 1600, prices rose perhaps five-fold. In England, if prices during the last half of the 15th century (before Columbus) are taken as 100, by the last decade of the 16th century they were roughly at 250; eighty years later, they were at around 350.

—*from John Kenneth Galbraith*, Money: Whence It Came, Where It Went

Money is good for bribing yourself through the inconveniences of life.

— *Gottfried Reinhardt, film producer*

Keep cool and collect.

— *Mae West*

The safest way to double your money is to fold it over once and put it in your pocket.

— *Frank McKinney "Kin" Hubbard, humorist*

Use it up, wear it out; Make it do, or do without.

— *New England maxim*

Annual income twenty pounds, annual expenditure nineteen six, result happiness. Annual income twenty pounds, annual expenditure twenty pounds ought and six, result misery.

— *Charles Dickens,* David Copperfield

Take care of the pence, and the pounds will take care of themselves.

— *William Lowndes, writer*

More and more I am certain that the only difference between man and animals is that men can count and animals cannot and if they count they mostly do count money.

— *Gertrude Stein,*
Everybody's Autobiography

I want to ask thee a solemn question. Did thee ever one single time have thy Bank book balance and thy own check book agree exactly?

— *Hannah Whitall Smith, letter to her sister, in Logan Pearsall Smith,*
Philadelphia Quaker

A miser grows rich by seeming poor: an extravagant man grows poor by seeming rich.

— *William Shakespeare*

Where large sums of money are concerned, it is advisable to trust nobody.

— *Agatha Christie*, Endless Night

I make money using my brains and lose money listening to my heart. But in the long run my books balance pretty well.

— *Kate Seredy*, The Singing Tree

Never invest your money in anything that eats or needs repairing.

— *Billy Rose*

A financier is a pawnbroker with imagination.

— *Arthur Pinero, dramatist*

Gone today, here tomorrow.

— *Catherine Crook De Camp, on retirement savings,* The Money Tree

Put not your trust in money, but put your money in trust.

— *Oliver Wendell Holmes,* The Autocrat of the Breakfast Table

A bank is a place that will lend you money if you don't need it.

— *Bob Hope,* The Tyranny of Farms

A bank is a place where they lend you an umbrella in fair weather and ask for it back again when it begins to rain.

— *Robert Frost*

A banker is a fellow who lends you his umbrella when the sun is shining and wants it back the minute it begins to rain.

— *Mark Twain*

In 1642, tobacco was made legal tender by the General Assembly of the colony of Virginia by outlawing contracts that called for payment in gold or silver.

—*from John Kenneth Galbraith,* Money: Whence It Came, Where It Went

Banking may well be a career from which no man really recovers.

—*John Kenneth Galbraith*

One rule which woe betides the banker who fails to heed it. . . . Never lend any money to anybody unless they don't need it.

— *Ogden Nash*

Banking establishments are more dangerous than standing armies.

— *Thomas Jefferson*

Bankers are just like anybody else, except richer.

— *Ogden Nash,*
"I Have It on Good Authority"

There have been three great inventions since the beginning of time: fire, the wheel, and central banking.

— *Will Rogers*

Money often costs too much.

— *Ralph Waldo Emerson*

One of the benefits of inflation is that kids can no longer get sick on a nickel's worth of candy.

— Journeyman Barber *magazine*

Invest in inflation. It is the only thing going up.

— *Will Rogers*

I don't know of anything more remorseless on the face of the earth than seven per cent interest.

— *Josh Billings, humorist*

Inflation is the one form of taxation that can be imposed without legislation.

— *Milton Friedman, economist*

Credit: a person who can't pay, gets another person who can't pay, to guarantee that he can pay.

— *Charles Dickens*

A creditor is worse than a master; for a master owns only your person, a creditor owns your dignity, and can belabor that.

— *Victor Hugo*

Business? It's quite simple. It's other people's money.

— *Alexandre Dumas the Younger,* La Question d'Argent

Live within your income, even if you have to borrow money to do so.

— *Josh Billings, humorist*

If you would like to know the value of money, go and try to borrow some.

— *Benjamin Franklin*

It is better to give than to lend and it costs about the same.

— *Philip Gibbs, journalist*

Credit buying is much like being drunk. The buzz happens immediately and gives you a lift. . . . The hangover comes the day after.

— *Dr. Joyce Brothers*

It is only the poor who pay cash, and that not from virtue, but because they are refused credit.

— *Anatole France*, A Cynic's Breviary

In general, the art of government consists in taking as much money as possible from one class of citizens to give to the other.

— *Voltaire,*
Dictionnaire Philosophique

The thing generally raised on city land is taxes.

— *Charles Dudley Warner, essayist*

The worst in the civilized world.

— *Andrew Carnegie, on the U.S. financial system*

In the early part of the 20th century, because the island yielded no metal, the medium of exchange used by inhabitants of Uap or Yap, a German colony in Micronesia, was fei, large solid stone wheels ranging in diameter from a foot to twelve feet, with a hole in the centre wherein a pole was inserted sufficiently large and strong to facilitate transporatation.

After concluding a bargain which involved the price of a fei too large to be conveniently moved, its new owner was quite content to accept the bare acknowledgement of ownership and without so much as a mark to indicate the exchange, the coin remains undisturbed on the former owner's premises.

—*from Milton Friedman,* Money Mischief

The hardest thing in the world to understand is the income tax.

—*Albert Einstein*

The income tax has made more liars out of the American people than gold has.

— *Will Rogers*

When there is an income tax, the just man will pay more and the unjust less on the same amount of income.

— *Plato*

The entire graduated income tax structure was created by Karl Marx.

— *Ronald Reagan*

Count that day won when, turning on its axis, this earth imposes no additional taxes.

— *Josh Billings, humorist*

Blessed are the young, for they shall inherit the national debt.

— *Herbert Hoover*

Any government, like any family, can for a year spend a little more than it earns. But you and I know that a continuance of that habit means the poorhouse.

— *Franklin Roosevelt*

The taxpayer—that's someone who works for the federal government but doesn't have to take a civil service exam.

— *Ronald Reagan*

There is no art which government sooner learns of another than that of draining money from the pockets of the people.

—*Adam Smith, economist*

Actually, if my business was legitimate, I would deduct a substantial percentage for depreciation of my body.

—*Xaviera Hollander*, The Happy Hooker

It is better to live rich than to die rich.

— *Samuel Johnson, in James Boswell,* Life of Johnson

The best way to attract money, she had discovered, was to give the appearance of having it.

— *Gail Sheehy,* Hustling

Leave off the agony, leave off style, / Unless you've got money by you all the while.

— *Julia A. Moore,* Leave off the Agony in Style

I, with my whimsied past, / spend my father's riches with caresses / and with a nimble swagger / scar the city with dreams.

— *Michael Ondaatje,* Paris

Nothing that costs only a dollar is worth having.

— *Elizabeth Arden, businesswoman*

Everything is worth what its purchaser will pay for it.

— *Pubilius Syrus*, Maxim 865

Man is the only creature that consumes without producing.

— *George Orwell*, Animal Farm

I'm sure the way to be happy is to live well beyond your means!

— *Ruth Gordon*, The Leading Lady

All progress is based upon a universal innate desire on the part of every organism to live beyond its income.

— *Samuel Butler*, Notebooks

Getting along with women, / Knocking around with men, / Having more credit than money, / Thus one goes through the world.

— *Johann Wolfgang von Goethe*,
Claudine von Villa Bella

I owe much; I have nothing; the rest I leave to the poor.

— *François Rabelais, writer*

There are only two classes in society: those who get more than they earn, and those who earn more than they get.

— *Holbrook Jackson, journalist*

A habit of debt is very injurious to the memory.

— *Austin O'Malley, oculist*

He is now fast rising from affluence to poverty.

— *Mark Twain*, Henry Ward Beecher's Farm

If making money is a slow process, losing it is quickly done.

— *Ihara Saikaku*, The Japanese Family Storehouse; or, The Millionaires' Gospel

Paying attention to simple little things that most men neglect makes a few men rich.

— *Henry Ford, industrialist*

That money talks/I'll not deny,/I heard it once:/It said, "Goodbye."

— *Richard Armour, writer*

Anyone who thinks there's safety in numbers hasn't looked at the stock market pages.

— *Irene Peter, writer*

Never ask of money spent/Where the spender thinks it went./Nobody was ever meant/To remember or invent/What he did with every cent.

— *Robert Frost*

A son can bear with equanimity the loss of his father, but the loss of his inheritance may drive him to despair.

— *Machiavelli,* The Prince

Hollywood money isn't money. It's congealed snow, melts in your hand, and there you are.

— *in Malcolm Cowley,* Writers at Work

These heroes of finance are like beads on a string—when one slips off, all the rest will follow.

— *Henrik Ibsen*

A big head and a big bank account don't keep company very long.

— *B.C. Forbes,* Epigrams

Lack of money is the root of all evil.

— *George Bernard Shaw*

A poor person who is unhappy is in a better position than a rich person who is unhappy. Because the poor person has hope. He thinks money would help.

— *Jean Kerr*, Poor Richard

The custom of depicting the head of the sovereign on coins began with Alexander the Great, not so much as a guarantee of their worth but as a personal gesture by the ruler to himself.

— *from John Kenneth Galbraith*, Money: Whence It Came, Where It Went

The trouble with being poor is that it takes up all your time.

— *William de Kooning*

There is no money in poetry, but then there is no poetry in money either.

— *Robert Graves*

There is nothing so degrading as the constant anxiety about one's means of livelihood.

— *W. Somerset Maugham,*
Of Human Bondage

Need of money, dear.

— *Dorothy Parker, writer, when asked about the source of most of her work*

Poor people who had escaped from poverty as I had, feared it, hated it, and fled from it all their lives. Those born rich could afford to be touched by it.

— *Anzia Yezierska, writer*

It is hard to be poor when there are so many rich fools at whose expense one could live.

— *Albert Camus,* Carnets

The rich rob the poor and the poor rob one another.

— *Sojourner Truth, suffragist*

Poverty of course is not a disgrace, but it is damned annoying.

— *William Pitt, British Prime Minister*

That's the definition of poverty. The less choice you have, the poorer you are.

— *Carrie Saxon Perry, politician*

I must say I hate money but it's the lack of it I hate most.

— *Katherine Mansfield, writer*

It's a kind of spiritual snobbery that makes people think they can be happy without money.

— *Albert Camus,* Notebooks 1935-1942

If Karl, instead of writing a lot about Capital, made a lot of Capital, it would have been much better.

— *Karl Marx's mother*

Few, save the poor, feel for the poor.

— Letitia Landon, "The Poor"

It's no disgrace t' be poor, but it might as well be.

— Frank McKinney "Kin" Hubbard, humorist

I'd like to live like a poor man with lots of money.

— Pablo Picasso

It was more than money that made me feel 'poor and deprived.' It was values.

— Ginny Berson, activist

The poor you have with you always—but they are not invited.

— Addison Mizner, architect

Boredom is the keynote of poverty . . . for where there is no money, there is no change of any kind, not of scene or of routine.

— *Moss Hart,* Act One

Money is always dull, except when you haven't got any, and then it's terrifying.

— *Sheila Bishop,*
The House with Two Faces

Those who never think of money need a great deal of it.

— *Agatha Christie,*
Witness for the Prosecution

He . . . knew now, more than ever, that money was everything, the wall that stood between all he loathed and all he wanted.

— *Willa Cather*, Youth and the Bright Aedusa

I am a poor man, but I have this consolation: I am poor by accident, not by design.

— *Josh Billings, humorist*

Come away, poverty's catching.

— *Aphra Behn*, The Rover

I've never been poor, only broke. Being poor is a frame of mind. Being broke is only a temporary situation.

— *Mike Todd, film producer*

Almost all the noblest things that have been achieved in the world have been achieved by poor men. A certain staidness and sobriety, a certain moderation and restraint, a certain pressure of circumstances are good for men. His body was not made for luxuries. It sickens, sinks, and dies under them.

— *Henry David Thoreau*

As a general rule, nobody has money who ought to have it.

— *Benjamin Disraeli*

We always come back to the same vicious circle—an extreme degree of material or intellectual poverty does away with the means of alleviating it.

— *Simone de Beauvoir*

How easy it is for a man to die rich, if he will but be contented to live miserable.

— *Henry Fielding*

Hunger steals the memory.

— *Louise Erdrich, writer*

Hunger also changes the world—when eating can't be a habit, then neither can seeing.

— *Maxine Hong Kingston, writer*

Hungry people cannot be good at learning or producing anything, except perhaps violence.

— *Pearl Bailey, singer*

A man with money to pay for a meal can talk about hunger without demeaning himself. But for a man with no money hunger is a disgrace.

— *Vicki Baum, writer*

It is an unfortunate human failing that a full pocketbook often groans more loudly than an empty stomach.

— *Franklin Roosevelt*

Any young man with good health and a poor appetite can save up money.

— *James Montgomery Bailey, journalist*

Eats first, morals after.

— *Bertolt Brecht*

Early to rise and early to bed makes a male healthy and wealthy and dead.
—*James Thurber*, Fables for Our Time

When I was young, I thought that money was the most important thing in life; now that I am old I know that it is.
— *Oscar Wilde*

You can be young without money but you can't be old without it.
— *Tennessee Williams*, Cat on a Hot Tin Roof

On August 15, 1971, U.S. president Richard Nixon "closed the gold window" by terminating the obligation that the United States had assumed to convert dollars held by foreign *monetary authorities into gold at the fixed price of $35 an ounce. Prior to 1971, every major currency from time immemorial had been linked directly or indirectly to a commodity.*

—*from Milton Friedman,* Money Mischief

Pay as you go, but not if you intend going for good.

—*James Jeffrey Roche, journalist*

So far I haven't heard of anyone who wants to stop living on the account of the cost.

— *Frank McKinney "Kin" Hubbard, humorist*

Money won't buy happiness, but it will pay the salaries of a large research staff to study the problem.

— *Bill Vaughn*

Money can't buy friends, but you can get a better class of enemy.

— *Spike Mulligan,* Puckoon

What is a thousand dollars? Mere chicken feed. A poultry matter.

— *Groucho Marx,*
The Cocoanuts

When a fellow says "It hain't the money but the principle o' the thing," it's th' money.

— *Frank McKinney "Kin" Hubbard,*
humorist

Money without honor is a disease.

— *Balzac*, Eugénie Grandet IV

Money differs from an automobile, a mistress, or cancer in being equally important to those who have it and those who do not.

— *John Kenneth Galbraith*

Money is a kind of poetry.

— *Wallace Stevens*, Opus Posthumous

Money is the string with which sardonic destiny directs the motions of its puppets.

— *W. Somerset Maugham*

Money is the wise man's religion.

— *Euripedes*

Money alone is the ruling principle of the world.

— *Henrik Ibsen*, Peer Gynt

Alle things obeyen to moneye.

— *Chaucer*, The Tales of Melibeus

SOURCES

Adams, A.K., ed. *The Home Book of Humorous Quotes*. New York: Dodd Mead & Co., 1969.

Adams, Abby. *An Uncommon Scold*. Simon and Schuster, 1989.

Andrews, Robert, ed. *Concise Columbia Dictionary of Quotations*. Columbia University Press, 1987.

Augarde, Tony, ed. *The Oxford Dictionary of Modern Quotations*. Oxford University Press, 1992.

Bunch, Charlotte and Nancy Myron, eds. *Class and Feminism*. Diana Press, 1944.

Charlton, James, ed. *The Executive's Quotation Book*. St. Martin's Press, 1983.

Collison, Robert and Mary, eds. *Dictionary of Foreign Quotations*. New York: Facts on File, 1980.

Colombo, John Robert, ed. *The Dictionary of Canadian Quotations*. Toronto: Stoddart, 1991.

Dworkin, Andrea. *Pornography: Men Possessing Women*. Perigree Books, 1979.

Esar, Evan, ed. *Dictionary of Humorous Quotations.* Bramhall House, n.d.

Evans, Bergen, ed. *Dictionary of Quotations.* New York: Delacourte, 1968.

Fuller, Edmund, ed. *Thesaurus of Epigrams.* New York: Garden City, 1948.

Hamilton, Robert M. and Dorothy Shields, eds. *The Dictionary of Canadian Quotations and Phrases.* Toronto: McClelland & Stewart, 1979.

Henry, Lewis C., ed. *Best Quotations for All Occasions.* Random House, 1955.

Kaplan, Justin, ed. *Bartlett's Familiar Quotations, 16th edition.* Little, Brown, 1992.

Maggio, Rosalie, ed. *The Beacon Book of Quotations by Women.* Beacon Press, 1992.

Partnow, Elaine, ed. *The Quotable Woman.* Vols. 1 and 2. Pinnacle Books, 1977.

Peter, Laurence J., ed. *Peter's Quotations: Ideas for Our Times.* William Morrow, 1977.

Simpson, James B., ed. *Simpson's Contemporary Quotations.* Boston: Houghton Mifflin, 1988.

Strickland, David, ed. *Quotations from English*

Canadian Literature. Toronto: Penguin, 1973.

Thematic Dictionary of Quotations. Bloomsbury, 1989.

Wolf, Naomi. *The Beauty Myth.* Random House, 1990.

INDEX

EVELYN STEINBERG is a principal and MARILYN WILLIAMS is a teacher working for the North York Board of Education in Ontario, Canada.

It is the purpose of Little Red Books to gather the essential wisdom of great women and men into single volumes so that students of the Great might judge them in light of their own words, and find where they will the spiritual, sporting, political, musical, and gardening models so earnestly sought after by the young, and so easily forgotten by the old.

LITTLE RED BOOKS

The Little Black & White Book of Film Noir
The Little Black Leather Book of Rock n Roll
The Little Blonde Book of Kim Campbell
The Little Blue Book of UFOs
The Little Book of Reform
The Little Book of Wrinkles
The Little Green Book
The Little Greenish-Brown Book of Slugs
The Little Grey Flannel Book
The Little Lavender Book
The Little Pink Pink
Quotations for a Nation
Quotations from Chairman Ballard
Quotations from Chairman Cherry
Quotations from Chairman Lamport
Quotations from Chairman Zalm
Quotations on the Great One
Viva Las Elvis